DAILY JOURNAL:
EASY AND QUICK FILL IN DIARY WITH DAILY QUESTIONS FOR MORE SELF-AWARENESS, SELF-LOVE, GRATITUDE, AND POSITIVITY
—
A DIN A5 NOTEBOOK TO HELP YOU CREATE MEANINGFUL DIARY ENTRIES, STICK TO DAILY DIARY WRITING ON A BUSY SCHEDULE, AND INCREASE YOUR PERSONAL GROWTH, HAPPINESS AND INNER PEACE

DAILY JOURNAL:
EASY AND QUICK FILL IN DIARY WITH DAILY QUESTIONS FOR MORE SELF-AWARENESS,
SELF-LOVE, GRATITUDE, AND POSITIVITY – A DIN A5 NOTEBOOK TO HELP YOU CREATE
MEANINGFUL DIARY ENTRIES, STICK TO DAILY DIARY WRITING ON A BUSY SCHEDULE, AND
INCREASE YOUR PERSONAL GROWTH, HAPPINESS AND INNER PEACE
FIRST EDITION

BIBLIOGRAFISCHE INFORMATION DER DEUTSCHEN NATIONALBIBLIOTHEK: DIE DEUTSCHE
NATIONALBIBLIOTHEK VERZEICHNET DIESE PUBLIKATION IN DER DEUTSCHEN
NATIONALBIBLIOGRAFIE; DETAILLIERTE BIBLIOGRAFISCHE DATEN SIND IM INTERNET ÜBER
DNB.DNB.DE ABRUFBAR.

©2022 ALINA BECKER
HERSTELLUNG UND VERLAG: BOD – BOOKS ON DEMAND, NORDERSTEDT

ISBN :9783756888108

A FEW WORDS
ABOUT
YOUR NEW
COMPANION:

THE 6 DAILY QUESTIONS:

1. WHAT DO YOUR MIND, BODY AND HEART NEED TODAY?
THIS IS NOT A TO-DO LIST.
IT´S AN I'M-AWARE-OF-WHAT-I-NEED LIST.

2. WHAT COULD BE YOUR REASON FOR HAPPINESS TODAY?

3. HOW CAN YOU SHOW SOME LOVE TO YOURSELF?

4. WHAT IS BOTHERING YOU?

5. WHAT CAN YOU CHANGE ABOUT IT TODAY?

6. WHAT DO YOU LIKE ABOUT YOURSELF?

THE DAILY SUMMARY:

SUMMARIZE YOUR DAY WITH A FEW WORDS OR PICTURES.
YOU CAN GO CRAZY OR KEEP IT SIMPLE.
HOWEVER YOU LIKE!

DATE | *Nov 19th 2022*

WHAT DOES MY ... NEED TODAY?

MIND — *To have a tidy apartment*

BODY — *Go for a run*

HEART — *Call Ann and tell her what's on my mind*

POSSIBLE ACT OF SELF-LOVE

I could practice some yoga today

TODAY'S REASON FOR HAPPINESS

To have such good friends that I can ALWAYS count on. I love them so much and am grateful to have them in my life

WHAT IS BOTHERING ME?

That I am chaotic. My flat looks so untidy...

WHAT TO DO ABOUT IT TODAY?

Today I'll clean and tidy up the living room. and I will turn the music UP (!), so I'll maybe even enjoy it

I LIKE ABOUT MYSELF THAT ...

I am strong

THE DAY IN A FEW WORDS

Morning: Yoga + nice music, enjoyed drinking my coffee
An adorable little girl waved and smiled at me on the bus. That was cute.
I was happy to meet Paul at work, we talked a lot and I felt guilty for starting work a little late. But it was worth it. He spreads so much positive energy.
Nice lunchbreak with Lea! We even went for a little walk after lunch☺
Working again - time passed quickly and I felt productive.
I got hooooome and continued reading my book,
cooked, had dinner and now I'm off to bed!

ENJOY YOUR JOURNEY.

DATE

WHAT DOES MY ...
NEED TODAY?

TODAY'S REASON FOR HAPPINESS

MIND

BODY

HEART

WHAT IS BOTHERING ME?

POSSIBLE
ACT OF SELF-LOVE

WHAT TO DO ABOUT IT TODAY?

I LIKE ABOUT MYSELF THAT ...

THE DAY IN A FEW WORDS

DATE

WHAT DOES MY ...
NEED TODAY?

TODAY'S REASON FOR HAPPINESS

MIND

BODY

HEART

WHAT IS BOTHERING ME?

POSSIBLE
ACT OF SELF-LOVE

WHAT TO DO ABOUT IT TODAY?

I LIKE ABOUT MYSELF THAT ...

THE DAY IN A FEW WORDS

DATE

WHAT DOES MY ...
NEED TODAY?

TODAY´S REASON FOR HAPPINESS

MIND

BODY

HEART

WHAT IS BOTHERING ME?

POSSIBLE
ACT OF SELF–LOVE

WHAT TO DO ABOUT IT TODAY?

I LIKE ABOUT MYSELF THAT ...

THE DAY IN A FEW WORDS

DATE

WHAT DOES MY ...
NEED TODAY?

TODAY´S REASON FOR HAPPINESS

MIND

BODY

HEART

WHAT IS BOTHERING ME?

POSSIBLE
ACT OF SELF-LOVE

WHAT TO DO ABOUT IT TODAY?

I LIKE ABOUT MYSELF THAT ...

THE DAY IN A FEW WORDS

DATE

WHAT DOES MY ...
NEED TODAY?

TODAY´S REASON FOR HAPPINESS

MIND

BODY

HEART

WHAT IS BOTHERING ME?

POSSIBLE
ACT OF SELF-LOVE

WHAT TO DO ABOUT IT TODAY?

I LIKE ABOUT MYSELF THAT ...

THE DAY IN A FEW WORDS

DATE

WHAT DOES MY ...
NEED TODAY?

TODAY´S REASON FOR HAPPINESS

MIND

BODY

HEART

WHAT IS BOTHERING ME?

POSSIBLE
ACT OF SELF—LOVE

WHAT TO DO ABOUT IT TODAY?

I LIKE ABOUT MYSELF THAT ...

THE DAY IN A FEW WORDS

DATE

WHAT DOES MY ...
NEED TODAY?

TODAY'S REASON FOR HAPPINESS

MIND

BODY

HEART

WHAT IS BOTHERING ME?

POSSIBLE
ACT OF SELF-LOVE

WHAT TO DO ABOUT IT TODAY?

I LIKE ABOUT MYSELF THAT ...

THE DAY IN A FEW WORDS

DATE

WHAT DOES MY ...
NEED TODAY?

TODAY'S REASON FOR HAPPINESS

MIND

BODY

HEART

WHAT IS BOTHERING ME?

POSSIBLE
ACT OF SELF—LOVE

WHAT TO DO ABOUT IT TODAY?

I LIKE ABOUT MYSELF THAT ...

THE DAY IN A FEW WORDS

DATE

WHAT DOES MY ...
NEED TODAY?

TODAY´S REASON FOR HAPPINESS

MIND

BODY

HEART

WHAT IS BOTHERING ME?

POSSIBLE
ACT OF SELF–LOVE

WHAT TO DO ABOUT IT TODAY?

I LIKE ABOUT MYSELF THAT ...

THE DAY IN A FEW WORDS

DATE

WHAT DOES MY ...
NEED TODAY?

TODAY´S REASON FOR HAPPINESS

MIND

BODY

HEART

WHAT IS BOTHERING ME?

POSSIBLE
ACT OF SELF—LOVE

WHAT TO DO ABOUT IT TODAY?

I LIKE ABOUT MYSELF THAT ...

THE DAY IN A FEW WORDS

DATE

WHAT DOES MY ...
NEED TODAY?

TODAY'S REASON FOR HAPPINESS

MIND

BODY

HEART

WHAT IS BOTHERING ME?

POSSIBLE
ACT OF SELF—LOVE

WHAT TO DO ABOUT IT TODAY?

I LIKE ABOUT MYSELF THAT ...

THE DAY IN A FEW WORDS

DATE

WHAT DOES MY ...
NEED TODAY?

TODAY'S REASON FOR HAPPINESS

MIND

BODY

HEART

WHAT IS BOTHERING ME?

POSSIBLE
ACT OF SELF-LOVE

WHAT TO DO ABOUT IT TODAY?

I LIKE ABOUT MYSELF THAT ...

THE DAY IN A FEW WORDS

DATE

WHAT DOES MY ...
NEED TODAY?

TODAY'S REASON FOR HAPPINESS

MIND

BODY

HEART

WHAT IS BOTHERING ME?

POSSIBLE
ACT OF SELF–LOVE

WHAT TO DO ABOUT IT TODAY?

I LIKE ABOUT MYSELF THAT ...

THE DAY IN A FEW WORDS

DATE

WHAT DOES MY ...
NEED TODAY?

TODAY'S REASON FOR HAPPINESS

MIND

BODY

HEART

WHAT IS BOTHERING ME?

POSSIBLE
ACT OF SELF-LOVE

WHAT TO DO ABOUT IT TODAY?

I LIKE ABOUT MYSELF THAT ...

THE DAY IN A FEW WORDS

DATE

WHAT DOES MY ...
NEED TODAY?

TODAY'S REASON FOR HAPPINESS

MIND

BODY

HEART

WHAT IS BOTHERING ME?

POSSIBLE
ACT OF SELF-LOVE

WHAT TO DO ABOUT IT TODAY?

I LIKE ABOUT MYSELF THAT ...

THE DAY IN A FEW WORDS

DATE

WHAT DOES MY ...
NEED TODAY?

MIND

BODY

HEART

POSSIBLE
ACT OF SELF-LOVE

TODAY´S REASON FOR HAPPINESS

WHAT IS BOTHERING ME?

WHAT TO DO ABOUT IT TODAY?

I LIKE ABOUT MYSELF THAT ...

THE DAY IN A FEW WORDS

DATE

WHAT DOES MY ...
NEED TODAY?

TODAY´S REASON FOR HAPPINESS

MIND

BODY

HEART

WHAT IS BOTHERING ME?

POSSIBLE
ACT OF SELF–LOVE

WHAT TO DO ABOUT IT TODAY?

I LIKE ABOUT MYSELF THAT ...

THE DAY IN A FEW WORDS

DATE

WHAT DOES MY ...
NEED TODAY?

TODAY'S REASON FOR HAPPINESS

MIND

BODY

HEART

WHAT IS BOTHERING ME?

POSSIBLE
ACT OF SELF-LOVE

WHAT TO DO ABOUT IT TODAY?

I LIKE ABOUT MYSELF THAT ...

THE DAY IN A FEW WORDS

DATE

WHAT DOES MY ...
NEED TODAY?

TODAY´S REASON FOR HAPPINESS

MIND

BODY

HEART

WHAT IS BOTHERING ME?

POSSIBLE
ACT OF SELF-LOVE

WHAT TO DO ABOUT IT TODAY?

I LIKE ABOUT MYSELF THAT ...

THE DAY IN A FEW WORDS

DATE

WHAT DOES MY ...
NEED TODAY?

TODAY'S REASON FOR HAPPINESS

MIND

BODY

HEART

WHAT IS BOTHERING ME?

POSSIBLE
ACT OF SELF–LOVE

WHAT TO DO ABOUT IT TODAY?

I LIKE ABOUT MYSELF THAT ...

THE DAY IN A FEW WORDS

DATE

WHAT DOES MY ...
NEED TODAY?

TODAY'S REASON FOR HAPPINESS

MIND

BODY

HEART

WHAT IS BOTHERING ME?

POSSIBLE
ACT OF SELF-LOVE

WHAT TO DO ABOUT IT TODAY?

I LIKE ABOUT MYSELF THAT ...

THE DAY IN A FEW WORDS

DATE

WHAT DOES MY ...
NEED TODAY?

TODAY´S REASON FOR HAPPINESS

MIND

BODY

HEART

WHAT IS BOTHERING ME?

POSSIBLE
ACT OF SELF-LOVE

WHAT TO DO ABOUT IT TODAY?

I LIKE ABOUT MYSELF THAT ...

THE DAY IN A FEW WORDS

DATE

WHAT DOES MY ...
NEED TODAY?

TODAY´S REASON FOR HAPPINESS

MIND

BODY

HEART

WHAT IS BOTHERING ME?

POSSIBLE
ACT OF SELF-LOVE

WHAT TO DO ABOUT IT TODAY?

I LIKE ABOUT MYSELF THAT ...

THE DAY IN A FEW WORDS

DATE

WHAT DOES MY ...
NEED TODAY?

TODAY´S REASON FOR HAPPINESS

MIND

BODY

HEART

WHAT IS BOTHERING ME?

POSSIBLE
ACT OF SELF-LOVE

WHAT TO DO ABOUT IT TODAY?

I LIKE ABOUT MYSELF THAT ...

THE DAY IN A FEW WORDS

DATE

WHAT DOES MY ...
NEED TODAY?

TODAY´S REASON FOR HAPPINESS

MIND

BODY

HEART

WHAT IS BOTHERING ME?

POSSIBLE
ACT OF SELF-LOVE

WHAT TO DO ABOUT IT TODAY?

I LIKE ABOUT MYSELF THAT ...

THE DAY IN A FEW WORDS

DATE

WHAT DOES MY ...
NEED TODAY?

TODAY´S REASON FOR HAPPINESS

MIND

BODY

HEART

WHAT IS BOTHERING ME?

POSSIBLE
ACT OF SELF–LOVE

WHAT TO DO ABOUT IT TODAY?

I LIKE ABOUT MYSELF THAT ...

THE DAY IN A FEW WORDS

DATE

WHAT DOES MY ...
NEED TODAY?

TODAY'S REASON FOR HAPPINESS

MIND

BODY

HEART

WHAT IS BOTHERING ME?

POSSIBLE
ACT OF SELF-LOVE

WHAT TO DO ABOUT IT TODAY?

I LIKE ABOUT MYSELF THAT ...

THE DAY IN A FEW WORDS

DATE

WHAT DOES MY ...
NEED TODAY?

MIND

BODY

HEART

POSSIBLE
ACT OF SELF-LOVE

TODAY'S REASON FOR HAPPINESS

WHAT IS BOTHERING ME?

WHAT TO DO ABOUT IT TODAY?

I LIKE ABOUT MYSELF THAT ...

THE DAY IN A FEW WORDS

DATE

WHAT DOES MY ...
NEED TODAY?

TODAY'S REASON FOR HAPPINESS

MIND

BODY

HEART

WHAT IS BOTHERING ME?

POSSIBLE
ACT OF SELF-LOVE

WHAT TO DO ABOUT IT TODAY?

I LIKE ABOUT MYSELF THAT ...

THE DAY IN A FEW WORDS

DATE ———

WHAT DOES MY ...
NEED TODAY?

TODAY´S REASON FOR HAPPINESS

MIND

BODY

HEART

WHAT IS BOTHERING ME?

POSSIBLE
ACT OF SELF–LOVE

WHAT TO DO ABOUT IT TODAY?

I LIKE ABOUT MYSELF THAT ...

THE DAY IN A FEW WORDS

DATE

WHAT DOES MY ...
NEED TODAY?

TODAY´S REASON FOR HAPPINESS

MIND

BODY

HEART

WHAT IS BOTHERING ME?

POSSIBLE
ACT OF SELF–LOVE

WHAT TO DO ABOUT IT TODAY?

I LIKE ABOUT MYSELF THAT ...

THE DAY IN A FEW WORDS

DATE

WHAT DOES MY ...
NEED TODAY?

TODAY'S REASON FOR HAPPINESS

MIND

BODY

HEART

WHAT IS BOTHERING ME?

POSSIBLE
ACT OF SELF-LOVE

WHAT TO DO ABOUT IT TODAY?

I LIKE ABOUT MYSELF THAT ...

THE DAY IN A FEW WORDS

DATE

WHAT DOES MY ...
NEED TODAY?

TODAY'S REASON FOR HAPPINESS

MIND

BODY

HEART

WHAT IS BOTHERING ME?

POSSIBLE
ACT OF SELF-LOVE

WHAT TO DO ABOUT IT TODAY?

I LIKE ABOUT MYSELF THAT ...

THE DAY IN A FEW WORDS

DATE

WHAT DOES MY ...
NEED TODAY?

TODAY´S REASON FOR HAPPINESS

MIND

BODY

HEART

WHAT IS BOTHERING ME?

POSSIBLE
ACT OF SELF–LOVE

WHAT TO DO ABOUT IT TODAY?

I LIKE ABOUT MYSELF THAT ...

THE DAY IN A FEW WORDS

DATE

WHAT DOES MY ...
NEED TODAY?

TODAY´S REASON FOR HAPPINESS

MIND

BODY

HEART

WHAT IS BOTHERING ME?

POSSIBLE
ACT OF SELF-LOVE

WHAT TO DO ABOUT IT TODAY?

I LIKE ABOUT MYSELF THAT ...

THE DAY IN A FEW WORDS

DATE

WHAT DOES MY ...
NEED TODAY?

TODAY'S REASON FOR HAPPINESS

MIND

BODY

HEART

WHAT IS BOTHERING ME?

POSSIBLE
ACT OF SELF–LOVE

WHAT TO DO ABOUT IT TODAY?

I LIKE ABOUT MYSELF THAT ...

THE DAY IN A FEW WORDS

DATE

WHAT DOES MY ...
NEED TODAY?

TODAY'S REASON FOR HAPPINESS

MIND

BODY

HEART

WHAT IS BOTHERING ME?

POSSIBLE
ACT OF SELF-LOVE

WHAT TO DO ABOUT IT TODAY?

I LIKE ABOUT MYSELF THAT ...

THE DAY IN A FEW WORDS

DATE

WHAT DOES MY ...
NEED TODAY?

TODAY'S REASON FOR HAPPINESS

MIND

BODY

HEART

WHAT IS BOTHERING ME?

POSSIBLE
ACT OF SELF-LOVE

WHAT TO DO ABOUT IT TODAY?

I LIKE ABOUT MYSELF THAT ...

THE DAY IN A FEW WORDS

DATE

WHAT DOES MY ...
NEED TODAY?

TODAY'S REASON FOR HAPPINESS

MIND

BODY

HEART

WHAT IS BOTHERING ME?

POSSIBLE
ACT OF SELF–LOVE

WHAT TO DO ABOUT IT TODAY?

I LIKE ABOUT MYSELF THAT ...

THE DAY IN A FEW WORDS

DATE

WHAT DOES MY ...
NEED TODAY?

TODAY'S REASON FOR HAPPINESS

MIND

BODY

HEART

WHAT IS BOTHERING ME?

POSSIBLE
ACT OF SELF-LOVE

WHAT TO DO ABOUT IT TODAY?

I LIKE ABOUT MYSELF THAT ...

THE DAY IN A FEW WORDS

DATE

WHAT DOES MY ...
NEED TODAY?

TODAY'S REASON FOR HAPPINESS

MIND

BODY

HEART

WHAT IS BOTHERING ME?

POSSIBLE
ACT OF SELF-LOVE

WHAT TO DO ABOUT IT TODAY?

I LIKE ABOUT MYSELF THAT ...

THE DAY IN A FEW WORDS

DATE

WHAT DOES MY ...
NEED TODAY?

TODAY´S REASON FOR HAPPINESS

MIND

BODY

HEART

WHAT IS BOTHERING ME?

POSSIBLE
ACT OF SELF−LOVE

WHAT TO DO ABOUT IT TODAY?

I LIKE ABOUT MYSELF THAT ...

THE DAY IN A FEW WORDS

DATE

WHAT DOES MY ...
NEED TODAY?

TODAY´S REASON FOR HAPPINESS

MIND

BODY

HEART

WHAT IS BOTHERING ME?

POSSIBLE
ACT OF SELF–LOVE

WHAT TO DO ABOUT IT TODAY?

I LIKE ABOUT MYSELF THAT ...

THE DAY IN A FEW WORDS

DATE

WHAT DOES MY ...
NEED TODAY?

TODAY'S REASON FOR HAPPINESS

MIND

BODY

HEART

WHAT IS BOTHERING ME?

POSSIBLE
ACT OF SELF-LOVE

WHAT TO DO ABOUT IT TODAY?

I LIKE ABOUT MYSELF THAT ...

THE DAY IN A FEW WORDS

DATE

WHAT DOES MY ...
NEED TODAY?

TODAY´S REASON FOR HAPPINESS

MIND

BODY

HEART

WHAT IS BOTHERING ME?

POSSIBLE
ACT OF SELF–LOVE

WHAT TO DO ABOUT IT TODAY?

I LIKE ABOUT MYSELF THAT ...

THE DAY IN A FEW WORDS

DATE

WHAT DOES MY ...
NEED TODAY?

TODAY´S REASON FOR HAPPINESS

MIND

BODY

HEART

WHAT IS BOTHERING ME?

POSSIBLE
ACT OF SELF–LOVE

WHAT TO DO ABOUT IT TODAY?

I LIKE ABOUT MYSELF THAT ...

THE DAY IN A FEW WORDS

DATE

WHAT DOES MY ...
NEED TODAY?

TODAY'S REASON FOR HAPPINESS

MIND

BODY

HEART

WHAT IS BOTHERING ME?

POSSIBLE
ACT OF SELF–LOVE

WHAT TO DO ABOUT IT TODAY?

I LIKE ABOUT MYSELF THAT ...

THE DAY IN A FEW WORDS

DATE

WHAT DOES MY ...
NEED TODAY?

TODAY´S REASON FOR HAPPINESS

MIND

BODY

HEART

WHAT IS BOTHERING ME?

POSSIBLE
ACT OF SELF–LOVE

WHAT TO DO ABOUT IT TODAY?

I LIKE ABOUT MYSELF THAT ...

THE DAY IN A FEW WORDS

DATE

WHAT DOES MY ...
NEED TODAY?

TODAY´S REASON FOR HAPPINESS

MIND

BODY

HEART

WHAT IS BOTHERING ME?

POSSIBLE
ACT OF SELF-LOVE

WHAT TO DO ABOUT IT TODAY?

I LIKE ABOUT MYSELF THAT ...

THE DAY IN A FEW WORDS

DATE

WHAT DOES MY ...
NEED TODAY?

TODAY´S REASON FOR HAPPINESS

MIND

BODY

HEART

WHAT IS BOTHERING ME?

POSSIBLE
ACT OF SELF−LOVE

WHAT TO DO ABOUT IT TODAY?

I LIKE ABOUT MYSELF THAT ...

THE DAY IN A FEW WORDS

DATE

WHAT DOES MY ...
NEED TODAY?

TODAY'S REASON FOR HAPPINESS

MIND

BODY

HEART

WHAT IS BOTHERING ME?

POSSIBLE
ACT OF SELF–LOVE

WHAT TO DO ABOUT IT TODAY?

I LIKE ABOUT MYSELF THAT ...

THE DAY IN A FEW WORDS

DATE

WHAT DOES MY ...
NEED TODAY?

TODAY'S REASON FOR HAPPINESS

MIND

BODY

HEART

WHAT IS BOTHERING ME?

POSSIBLE
ACT OF SELF-LOVE

WHAT TO DO ABOUT IT TODAY?

I LIKE ABOUT MYSELF THAT ...

THE DAY IN A FEW WORDS

DATE

WHAT DOES MY ...
NEED TODAY?

TODAY´S REASON FOR HAPPINESS

MIND

BODY

HEART

WHAT IS BOTHERING ME?

POSSIBLE
ACT OF SELF-LOVE

WHAT TO DO ABOUT IT TODAY?

I LIKE ABOUT MYSELF THAT ...

THE DAY IN A FEW WORDS

DATE

WHAT DOES MY ...
NEED TODAY?

TODAY'S REASON FOR HAPPINESS

MIND

BODY

HEART

WHAT IS BOTHERING ME?

POSSIBLE
ACT OF SELF—LOVE

WHAT TO DO ABOUT IT TODAY?

I LIKE ABOUT MYSELF THAT ...

THE DAY IN A FEW WORDS

DATE

WHAT DOES MY ...
NEED TODAY?

TODAY´S REASON FOR HAPPINESS

MIND

BODY

HEART

WHAT IS BOTHERING ME?

POSSIBLE
ACT OF SELF–LOVE

WHAT TO DO ABOUT IT TODAY?

I LIKE ABOUT MYSELF THAT ...

THE DAY IN A FEW WORDS

DATE

WHAT DOES MY ...
NEED TODAY?

TODAY´S REASON FOR HAPPINESS

MIND

BODY

HEART

WHAT IS BOTHERING ME?

POSSIBLE
ACT OF SELF–LOVE

WHAT TO DO ABOUT IT TODAY?

I LIKE ABOUT MYSELF THAT ...

THE DAY IN A FEW WORDS

DATE

WHAT DOES MY ...
NEED TODAY?

TODAY'S REASON FOR HAPPINESS

MIND

BODY

HEART

WHAT IS BOTHERING ME?

POSSIBLE
ACT OF SELF-LOVE

WHAT TO DO ABOUT IT TODAY?

I LIKE ABOUT MYSELF THAT ...

THE DAY IN A FEW WORDS

DATE

WHAT DOES MY ...
NEED TODAY?

TODAY'S REASON FOR HAPPINESS

MIND

BODY

HEART

WHAT IS BOTHERING ME?

POSSIBLE
ACT OF SELF—LOVE

WHAT TO DO ABOUT IT TODAY?

I LIKE ABOUT MYSELF THAT ...

THE DAY IN A FEW WORDS

DATE

WHAT DOES MY ...
NEED TODAY?

TODAY'S REASON FOR HAPPINESS

MIND

BODY

HEART

WHAT IS BOTHERING ME?

POSSIBLE
ACT OF SELF—LOVE

WHAT TO DO ABOUT IT TODAY?

I LIKE ABOUT MYSELF THAT ...

THE DAY IN A FEW WORDS

DATE

WHAT DOES MY ...
NEED TODAY?

TODAY'S REASON FOR HAPPINESS

MIND

BODY

HEART

WHAT IS BOTHERING ME?

POSSIBLE
ACT OF SELF-LOVE

WHAT TO DO ABOUT IT TODAY?

I LIKE ABOUT MYSELF THAT ...

THE DAY IN A FEW WORDS

DATE

WHAT DOES MY ...
NEED TODAY?

TODAY'S REASON FOR HAPPINESS

MIND

BODY

HEART

WHAT IS BOTHERING ME?

POSSIBLE
ACT OF SELF-LOVE

WHAT TO DO ABOUT IT TODAY?

I LIKE ABOUT MYSELF THAT ...

THE DAY IN A FEW WORDS

DATE

WHAT DOES MY ...
NEED TODAY?

TODAY´S REASON FOR HAPPINESS

MIND

BODY

HEART

WHAT IS BOTHERING ME?

POSSIBLE
ACT OF SELF-LOVE

WHAT TO DO ABOUT IT TODAY?

I LIKE ABOUT MYSELF THAT ...

THE DAY IN A FEW WORDS

DATE

WHAT DOES MY ...
NEED TODAY?

TODAY'S REASON FOR HAPPINESS

MIND

BODY

HEART

WHAT IS BOTHERING ME?

POSSIBLE
ACT OF SELF–LOVE

WHAT TO DO ABOUT IT TODAY?

I LIKE ABOUT MYSELF THAT ...

THE DAY IN A FEW WORDS

DATE

WHAT DOES MY ...
NEED TODAY?

TODAY'S REASON FOR HAPPINESS

MIND

BODY

HEART

WHAT IS BOTHERING ME?

POSSIBLE
ACT OF SELF-LOVE

WHAT TO DO ABOUT IT TODAY?

I LIKE ABOUT MYSELF THAT ...

THE DAY IN A FEW WORDS

DATE

WHAT DOES MY ...
NEED TODAY?

TODAY´S REASON FOR HAPPINESS

MIND

BODY

HEART

WHAT IS BOTHERING ME?

POSSIBLE
ACT OF SELF–LOVE

WHAT TO DO ABOUT IT TODAY?

I LIKE ABOUT MYSELF THAT ...

THE DAY IN A FEW WORDS

DATE

WHAT DOES MY ...
NEED TODAY?

TODAY'S REASON FOR HAPPINESS

MIND

BODY

HEART

WHAT IS BOTHERING ME?

POSSIBLE
ACT OF SELF—LOVE

WHAT TO DO ABOUT IT TODAY?

I LIKE ABOUT MYSELF THAT ...

THE DAY IN A FEW WORDS

DATE

WHAT DOES MY ...
NEED TODAY?

TODAY'S REASON FOR HAPPINESS

MIND

BODY

HEART

WHAT IS BOTHERING ME?

POSSIBLE
ACT OF SELF-LOVE

WHAT TO DO ABOUT IT TODAY?

I LIKE ABOUT MYSELF THAT ...

THE DAY IN A FEW WORDS

DATE

WHAT DOES MY ...
NEED TODAY?

MIND

BODY

HEART

POSSIBLE
ACT OF SELF–LOVE

TODAY'S REASON FOR HAPPINESS

WHAT IS BOTHERING ME?

WHAT TO DO ABOUT IT TODAY?

I LIKE ABOUT MYSELF THAT ...

THE DAY IN A FEW WORDS

DATE

WHAT DOES MY ...
NEED TODAY?

TODAY´S REASON FOR HAPPINESS

MIND

BODY

HEART

WHAT IS BOTHERING ME?

POSSIBLE
ACT OF SELF–LOVE

WHAT TO DO ABOUT IT TODAY?

I LIKE ABOUT MYSELF THAT ...

THE DAY IN A FEW WORDS

DATE

WHAT DOES MY ...
NEED TODAY?

TODAY´S REASON FOR HAPPINESS

MIND

BODY

HEART

WHAT IS BOTHERING ME?

POSSIBLE
ACT OF SELF–LOVE

WHAT TO DO ABOUT IT TODAY?

I LIKE ABOUT MYSELF THAT ...

THE DAY IN A FEW WORDS

DATE

WHAT DOES MY ...
NEED TODAY?

TODAY´S REASON FOR HAPPINESS

MIND

BODY

HEART

WHAT IS BOTHERING ME?

POSSIBLE
ACT OF SELF–LOVE

WHAT TO DO ABOUT IT TODAY?

I LIKE ABOUT MYSELF THAT ...

THE DAY IN A FEW WORDS

DATE

WHAT DOES MY ...
NEED TODAY?

TODAY'S REASON FOR HAPPINESS

MIND

BODY

HEART

WHAT IS BOTHERING ME?

POSSIBLE
ACT OF SELF—LOVE

WHAT TO DO ABOUT IT TODAY?

I LIKE ABOUT MYSELF THAT ...

THE DAY IN A FEW WORDS

DATE

WHAT DOES MY ...
NEED TODAY?

TODAY'S REASON FOR HAPPINESS

MIND

BODY

HEART

WHAT IS BOTHERING ME?

POSSIBLE
ACT OF SELF-LOVE

WHAT TO DO ABOUT IT TODAY?

I LIKE ABOUT MYSELF THAT ...

THE DAY IN A FEW WORDS

DATE

WHAT DOES MY ...
NEED TODAY?

TODAY´S REASON FOR HAPPINESS

MIND

BODY

HEART

WHAT IS BOTHERING ME?

POSSIBLE
ACT OF SELF—LOVE

WHAT TO DO ABOUT IT TODAY?

I LIKE ABOUT MYSELF THAT ...

THE DAY IN A FEW WORDS

DATE

WHAT DOES MY ...
NEED TODAY?

TODAY'S REASON FOR HAPPINESS

MIND

BODY

HEART

WHAT IS BOTHERING ME?

POSSIBLE
ACT OF SELF–LOVE

WHAT TO DO ABOUT IT TODAY?

I LIKE ABOUT MYSELF THAT ...

THE DAY IN A FEW WORDS

DATE

WHAT DOES MY ...
NEED TODAY?

TODAY'S REASON FOR HAPPINESS

MIND

BODY

HEART

WHAT IS BOTHERING ME?

POSSIBLE
ACT OF SELF-LOVE

WHAT TO DO ABOUT IT TODAY?

I LIKE ABOUT MYSELF THAT ...

THE DAY IN A FEW WORDS

DATE

WHAT DOES MY ...
NEED TODAY?

TODAY'S REASON FOR HAPPINESS

MIND

BODY

HEART

WHAT IS BOTHERING ME?

POSSIBLE
ACT OF SELF-LOVE

WHAT TO DO ABOUT IT TODAY?

I LIKE ABOUT MYSELF THAT ...

THE DAY IN A FEW WORDS

DATE

WHAT DOES MY ...
NEED TODAY?

TODAY'S REASON FOR HAPPINESS

MIND

BODY

HEART

WHAT IS BOTHERING ME?

POSSIBLE
ACT OF SELF–LOVE

WHAT TO DO ABOUT IT TODAY?

I LIKE ABOUT MYSELF THAT ...

THE DAY IN A FEW WORDS

DATE

WHAT DOES MY ...
NEED TODAY?

TODAY´S REASON FOR HAPPINESS

MIND

BODY

HEART

WHAT IS BOTHERING ME?

POSSIBLE
ACT OF SELF–LOVE

WHAT TO DO ABOUT IT TODAY?

I LIKE ABOUT MYSELF THAT ...

THE DAY IN A FEW WORDS

LOOK HOW FAR YOU'VE COME

DATE

WHAT DOES MY ...
NEED TODAY?

TODAY'S REASON FOR HAPPINESS

MIND

BODY

HEART

WHAT IS BOTHERING ME?

POSSIBLE
ACT OF SELF-LOVE

WHAT TO DO ABOUT IT TODAY?

I LIKE ABOUT MYSELF THAT ...

THE DAY IN A FEW WORDS

DATE

WHAT DOES MY ...
NEED TODAY?

TODAY´S REASON FOR HAPPINESS

MIND

BODY

HEART

WHAT IS BOTHERING ME?

POSSIBLE
ACT OF SELF-LOVE

WHAT TO DO ABOUT IT TODAY?

I LIKE ABOUT MYSELF THAT ...

THE DAY IN A FEW WORDS

DATE

WHAT DOES MY ...
NEED TODAY?

TODAY'S REASON FOR HAPPINESS

MIND

BODY

HEART

WHAT IS BOTHERING ME?

POSSIBLE
ACT OF SELF-LOVE

WHAT TO DO ABOUT IT TODAY?

I LIKE ABOUT MYSELF THAT ...

THE DAY IN A FEW WORDS

DATE

WHAT DOES MY ...
NEED TODAY?

TODAY'S REASON FOR HAPPINESS

MIND

BODY

HEART

WHAT IS BOTHERING ME?

POSSIBLE
ACT OF SELF—LOVE

WHAT TO DO ABOUT IT TODAY?

I LIKE ABOUT MYSELF THAT ...

THE DAY IN A FEW WORDS

DATE

WHAT DOES MY ...
NEED TODAY?

TODAY´S REASON FOR HAPPINESS

MIND

BODY

HEART

WHAT IS BOTHERING ME?

POSSIBLE
ACT OF SELF−LOVE

WHAT TO DO ABOUT IT TODAY?

I LIKE ABOUT MYSELF THAT ...

THE DAY IN A FEW WORDS

DATE

WHAT DOES MY ...
NEED TODAY?

TODAY'S REASON FOR HAPPINESS

MIND

BODY

HEART

WHAT IS BOTHERING ME?

POSSIBLE
ACT OF SELF-LOVE

WHAT TO DO ABOUT IT TODAY?

I LIKE ABOUT MYSELF THAT ...

THE DAY IN A FEW WORDS

DATE

WHAT DOES MY ...
NEED TODAY?

TODAY'S REASON FOR HAPPINESS

MIND

BODY

HEART

WHAT IS BOTHERING ME?

POSSIBLE
ACT OF SELF–LOVE

WHAT TO DO ABOUT IT TODAY?

I LIKE ABOUT MYSELF THAT ...

THE DAY IN A FEW WORDS

DATE

WHAT DOES MY ...
NEED TODAY?

TODAY'S REASON FOR HAPPINESS

MIND

BODY

HEART

WHAT IS BOTHERING ME?

POSSIBLE
ACT OF SELF-LOVE

WHAT TO DO ABOUT IT TODAY?

I LIKE ABOUT MYSELF THAT ...

THE DAY IN A FEW WORDS

DATE

WHAT DOES MY ...
NEED TODAY?

TODAY´S REASON FOR HAPPINESS

MIND

BODY

HEART

WHAT IS BOTHERING ME?

POSSIBLE
ACT OF SELF–LOVE

WHAT TO DO ABOUT IT TODAY?

I LIKE ABOUT MYSELF THAT ...

THE DAY IN A FEW WORDS

DATE

WHAT DOES MY ...
NEED TODAY?

TODAY'S REASON FOR HAPPINESS

MIND

BODY

HEART

WHAT IS BOTHERING ME?

POSSIBLE
ACT OF SELF—LOVE

WHAT TO DO ABOUT IT TODAY?

I LIKE ABOUT MYSELF THAT ...

THE DAY IN A FEW WORDS

DATE

WHAT DOES MY ...
NEED TODAY?

TODAY´S REASON FOR HAPPINESS

MIND

BODY

HEART

WHAT IS BOTHERING ME?

POSSIBLE
ACT OF SELF–LOVE

WHAT TO DO ABOUT IT TODAY?

I LIKE ABOUT MYSELF THAT ...

THE DAY IN A FEW WORDS

DATE

WHAT DOES MY ...
NEED TODAY?

TODAY'S REASON FOR HAPPINESS

MIND

BODY

HEART

WHAT IS BOTHERING ME?

POSSIBLE
ACT OF SELF-LOVE

WHAT TO DO ABOUT IT TODAY?

I LIKE ABOUT MYSELF THAT ...

THE DAY IN A FEW WORDS

DATE

WHAT DOES MY ...
NEED TODAY?

TODAY'S REASON FOR HAPPINESS

MIND

BODY

HEART

WHAT IS BOTHERING ME?

POSSIBLE
ACT OF SELF–LOVE

WHAT TO DO ABOUT IT TODAY?

I LIKE ABOUT MYSELF THAT ...

THE DAY IN A FEW WORDS

DATE

WHAT DOES MY ...
NEED TODAY?

TODAY´S REASON FOR HAPPINESS

MIND

BODY

HEART

WHAT IS BOTHERING ME?

POSSIBLE
ACT OF SELF–LOVE

WHAT TO DO ABOUT IT TODAY?

I LIKE ABOUT MYSELF THAT ...

THE DAY IN A FEW WORDS

DATE

WHAT DOES MY ...
NEED TODAY?

TODAY´S REASON FOR HAPPINESS

MIND

BODY

HEART

WHAT IS BOTHERING ME?

POSSIBLE
ACT OF SELF–LOVE

WHAT TO DO ABOUT IT TODAY?

I LIKE ABOUT MYSELF THAT ...

THE DAY IN A FEW WORDS

DATE

WHAT DOES MY ...
NEED TODAY?

TODAY'S REASON FOR HAPPINESS

MIND

BODY

HEART

WHAT IS BOTHERING ME?

POSSIBLE
ACT OF SELF–LOVE

WHAT TO DO ABOUT IT TODAY?

I LIKE ABOUT MYSELF THAT ...

THE DAY IN A FEW WORDS

DATE

WHAT DOES MY ...
NEED TODAY?

TODAY´S REASON FOR HAPPINESS

MIND

BODY

HEART

WHAT IS BOTHERING ME?

POSSIBLE
ACT OF SELF-LOVE

WHAT TO DO ABOUT IT TODAY?

I LIKE ABOUT MYSELF THAT ...

THE DAY IN A FEW WORDS

DATE

WHAT DOES MY ...
NEED TODAY?

TODAY'S REASON FOR HAPPINESS

MIND

BODY

HEART

WHAT IS BOTHERING ME?

POSSIBLE
ACT OF SELF-LOVE

WHAT TO DO ABOUT IT TODAY?

I LIKE ABOUT MYSELF THAT ...

THE DAY IN A FEW WORDS

DATE

WHAT DOES MY ...
NEED TODAY?

TODAY'S REASON FOR HAPPINESS

MIND

BODY

HEART

WHAT IS BOTHERING ME?

POSSIBLE
ACT OF SELF–LOVE

WHAT TO DO ABOUT IT TODAY?

I LIKE ABOUT MYSELF THAT ...

THE DAY IN A FEW WORDS

DATE

WHAT DOES MY ...
NEED TODAY?

TODAY'S REASON FOR HAPPINESS

MIND

BODY

HEART

WHAT IS BOTHERING ME?

POSSIBLE
ACT OF SELF-LOVE

WHAT TO DO ABOUT IT TODAY?

I LIKE ABOUT MYSELF THAT ...

THE DAY IN A FEW WORDS

DATE

WHAT DOES MY ...
NEED TODAY?

TODAY'S REASON FOR HAPPINESS

MIND

BODY

HEART

WHAT IS BOTHERING ME?

POSSIBLE
ACT OF SELF-LOVE

WHAT TO DO ABOUT IT TODAY?

I LIKE ABOUT MYSELF THAT ...

THE DAY IN A FEW WORDS

DATE

WHAT DOES MY ...
NEED TODAY?

TODAY'S REASON FOR HAPPINESS

MIND

BODY

HEART

WHAT IS BOTHERING ME?

POSSIBLE
ACT OF SELF–LOVE

WHAT TO DO ABOUT IT TODAY?

I LIKE ABOUT MYSELF THAT ...

THE DAY IN A FEW WORDS

DATE

WHAT DOES MY ...
NEED TODAY?

TODAY'S REASON FOR HAPPINESS

MIND

BODY

HEART

WHAT IS BOTHERING ME?

POSSIBLE
ACT OF SELF-LOVE

WHAT TO DO ABOUT IT TODAY?

I LIKE ABOUT MYSELF THAT ...

THE DAY IN A FEW WORDS

DATE

WHAT DOES MY ...
NEED TODAY?

TODAY'S REASON FOR HAPPINESS

MIND

BODY

HEART

WHAT IS BOTHERING ME?

POSSIBLE
ACT OF SELF-LOVE

WHAT TO DO ABOUT IT TODAY?

I LIKE ABOUT MYSELF THAT ...

THE DAY IN A FEW WORDS

DATE

WHAT DOES MY ...
NEED TODAY?

TODAY'S REASON FOR HAPPINESS

MIND

BODY

HEART

WHAT IS BOTHERING ME?

POSSIBLE
ACT OF SELF–LOVE

WHAT TO DO ABOUT IT TODAY?

I LIKE ABOUT MYSELF THAT ...

THE DAY IN A FEW WORDS

DATE

WHAT DOES MY ...
NEED TODAY?

TODAY'S REASON FOR HAPPINESS

MIND

BODY

HEART

WHAT IS BOTHERING ME?

POSSIBLE
ACT OF SELF—LOVE

WHAT TO DO ABOUT IT TODAY?

I LIKE ABOUT MYSELF THAT ...

THE DAY IN A FEW WORDS

DATE

WHAT DOES MY ...
NEED TODAY?

TODAY'S REASON FOR HAPPINESS

MIND

BODY

HEART

WHAT IS BOTHERING ME?

POSSIBLE
ACT OF SELF-LOVE

WHAT TO DO ABOUT IT TODAY?

I LIKE ABOUT MYSELF THAT ...

THE DAY IN A FEW WORDS

DATE

WHAT DOES MY ...
NEED TODAY?

TODAY'S REASON FOR HAPPINESS

MIND

BODY

HEART

WHAT IS BOTHERING ME?

POSSIBLE
ACT OF SELF-LOVE

WHAT TO DO ABOUT IT TODAY?

I LIKE ABOUT MYSELF THAT ...

THE DAY IN A FEW WORDS

DATE

WHAT DOES MY ...
NEED TODAY?

TODAY´S REASON FOR HAPPINESS

MIND

BODY

HEART

WHAT IS BOTHERING ME?

POSSIBLE
ACT OF SELF-LOVE

WHAT TO DO ABOUT IT TODAY?

I LIKE ABOUT MYSELF THAT ...

THE DAY IN A FEW WORDS

DATE

WHAT DOES MY ...
NEED TODAY?

TODAY'S REASON FOR HAPPINESS

MIND

BODY

HEART

WHAT IS BOTHERING ME?

POSSIBLE
ACT OF SELF-LOVE

WHAT TO DO ABOUT IT TODAY?

I LIKE ABOUT MYSELF THAT ...

THE DAY IN A FEW WORDS

DATE

WHAT DOES MY ...
NEED TODAY?

TODAY´S REASON FOR HAPPINESS

MIND

BODY

HEART

WHAT IS BOTHERING ME?

POSSIBLE
ACT OF SELF-LOVE

WHAT TO DO ABOUT IT TODAY?

I LIKE ABOUT MYSELF THAT ...

THE DAY IN A FEW WORDS

DATE

WHAT DOES MY ...
NEED TODAY?

TODAY'S REASON FOR HAPPINESS

MIND

BODY

HEART

WHAT IS BOTHERING ME?

POSSIBLE
ACT OF SELF-LOVE

WHAT TO DO ABOUT IT TODAY?

I LIKE ABOUT MYSELF THAT ...

THE DAY IN A FEW WORDS

DATE

WHAT DOES MY ...
NEED TODAY?

TODAY'S REASON FOR HAPPINESS

MIND

BODY

HEART

WHAT IS BOTHERING ME?

POSSIBLE
ACT OF SELF-LOVE

WHAT TO DO ABOUT IT TODAY?

I LIKE ABOUT MYSELF THAT ...

THE DAY IN A FEW WORDS

DATE

WHAT DOES MY ...
NEED TODAY?

TODAY'S REASON FOR HAPPINESS

MIND

BODY

HEART

WHAT IS BOTHERING ME?

POSSIBLE
ACT OF SELF-LOVE

WHAT TO DO ABOUT IT TODAY?

I LIKE ABOUT MYSELF THAT ...

THE DAY IN A FEW WORDS

DATE

WHAT DOES MY ...
NEED TODAY?

TODAY´S REASON FOR HAPPINESS

MIND

BODY

HEART

WHAT IS BOTHERING ME?

POSSIBLE
ACT OF SELF-LOVE

WHAT TO DO ABOUT IT TODAY?

I LIKE ABOUT MYSELF THAT ...

THE DAY IN A FEW WORDS

DATE

WHAT DOES MY ...
NEED TODAY?

TODAY'S REASON FOR HAPPINESS

MIND

BODY

HEART

WHAT IS BOTHERING ME?

POSSIBLE
ACT OF SELF−LOVE

WHAT TO DO ABOUT IT TODAY?

I LIKE ABOUT MYSELF THAT ...

THE DAY IN A FEW WORDS

DATE

WHAT DOES MY ...
NEED TODAY?

TODAY´S REASON FOR HAPPINESS

MIND

BODY

HEART

WHAT IS BOTHERING ME?

POSSIBLE
ACT OF SELF–LOVE

WHAT TO DO ABOUT IT TODAY?

I LIKE ABOUT MYSELF THAT ...

THE DAY IN A FEW WORDS

DATE

WHAT DOES MY ...
NEED TODAY?

TODAY'S REASON FOR HAPPINESS

MIND

BODY

HEART

WHAT IS BOTHERING ME?

POSSIBLE
ACT OF SELF-LOVE

WHAT TO DO ABOUT IT TODAY?

I LIKE ABOUT MYSELF THAT ...

THE DAY IN A FEW WORDS

DATE

WHAT DOES MY ...
NEED TODAY?

TODAY'S REASON FOR HAPPINESS

MIND

BODY

HEART

WHAT IS BOTHERING ME?

POSSIBLE
ACT OF SELF-LOVE

WHAT TO DO ABOUT IT TODAY?

I LIKE ABOUT MYSELF THAT ...

THE DAY IN A FEW WORDS

DATE

WHAT DOES MY ...
NEED TODAY?

TODAY´S REASON FOR HAPPINESS

MIND

BODY

HEART

WHAT IS BOTHERING ME?

POSSIBLE
ACT OF SELF–LOVE

WHAT TO DO ABOUT IT TODAY?

I LIKE ABOUT MYSELF THAT ...

THE DAY IN A FEW WORDS

DATE

WHAT DOES MY ...
NEED TODAY?

TODAY'S REASON FOR HAPPINESS

MIND

BODY

HEART

WHAT IS BOTHERING ME?

POSSIBLE
ACT OF SELF-LOVE

WHAT TO DO ABOUT IT TODAY?

I LIKE ABOUT MYSELF THAT ...

THE DAY IN A FEW WORDS

DATE

WHAT DOES MY ...
NEED TODAY?

TODAY'S REASON FOR HAPPINESS

MIND

BODY

HEART

WHAT IS BOTHERING ME?

POSSIBLE
ACT OF SELF-LOVE

WHAT TO DO ABOUT IT TODAY?

I LIKE ABOUT MYSELF THAT ...

THE DAY IN A FEW WORDS

DATE

WHAT DOES MY ...
NEED TODAY?

TODAY´S REASON FOR HAPPINESS

MIND

BODY

HEART

WHAT IS BOTHERING ME?

POSSIBLE
ACT OF SELF–LOVE

WHAT TO DO ABOUT IT TODAY?

I LIKE ABOUT MYSELF THAT ...

THE DAY IN A FEW WORDS

DATE

WHAT DOES MY ...
NEED TODAY?

MIND

BODY

HEART

POSSIBLE
ACT OF SELF—LOVE

TODAY'S REASON FOR HAPPINESS

WHAT IS BOTHERING ME?

WHAT TO DO ABOUT IT TODAY?

I LIKE ABOUT MYSELF THAT ...

THE DAY IN A FEW WORDS

DATE

WHAT DOES MY ...
NEED TODAY?

TODAY´S REASON FOR HAPPINESS

MIND

BODY

HEART

WHAT IS BOTHERING ME?

POSSIBLE
ACT OF SELF–LOVE

WHAT TO DO ABOUT IT TODAY?

I LIKE ABOUT MYSELF THAT ...

THE DAY IN A FEW WORDS

DATE

WHAT DOES MY ...
NEED TODAY?

TODAY'S REASON FOR HAPPINESS

MIND

BODY

HEART

WHAT IS BOTHERING ME?

POSSIBLE
ACT OF SELF–LOVE

WHAT TO DO ABOUT IT TODAY?

I LIKE ABOUT MYSELF THAT ...

THE DAY IN A FEW WORDS

DATE

WHAT DOES MY ...
NEED TODAY?

TODAY'S REASON FOR HAPPINESS

MIND

BODY

HEART

WHAT IS BOTHERING ME?

POSSIBLE
ACT OF SELF-LOVE

WHAT TO DO ABOUT IT TODAY?

I LIKE ABOUT MYSELF THAT ...

THE DAY IN A FEW WORDS

DATE

WHAT DOES MY ...
NEED TODAY?

TODAY'S REASON FOR HAPPINESS

MIND

BODY

HEART

WHAT IS BOTHERING ME?

POSSIBLE
ACT OF SELF-LOVE

WHAT TO DO ABOUT IT TODAY?

I LIKE ABOUT MYSELF THAT ...

THE DAY IN A FEW WORDS

DATE

WHAT DOES MY ...
NEED TODAY?

TODAY'S REASON FOR HAPPINESS

MIND

BODY

HEART

WHAT IS BOTHERING ME?

POSSIBLE
ACT OF SELF-LOVE

WHAT TO DO ABOUT IT TODAY?

I LIKE ABOUT MYSELF THAT ...

THE DAY IN A FEW WORDS

DATE

WHAT DOES MY ...
NEED TODAY?

TODAY'S REASON FOR HAPPINESS

MIND

BODY

HEART

WHAT IS BOTHERING ME?

POSSIBLE
ACT OF SELF—LOVE

WHAT TO DO ABOUT IT TODAY?

I LIKE ABOUT MYSELF THAT ...

THE DAY IN A FEW WORDS

DATE

WHAT DOES MY ...
NEED TODAY?

TODAY'S REASON FOR HAPPINESS

MIND

BODY

HEART

WHAT IS BOTHERING ME?

POSSIBLE
ACT OF SELF–LOVE

WHAT TO DO ABOUT IT TODAY?

I LIKE ABOUT MYSELF THAT ...

THE DAY IN A FEW WORDS

DATE

WHAT DOES MY ...
NEED TODAY?

TODAY'S REASON FOR HAPPINESS

MIND

BODY

HEART

WHAT IS BOTHERING ME?

POSSIBLE
ACT OF SELF-LOVE

WHAT TO DO ABOUT IT TODAY?

I LIKE ABOUT MYSELF THAT ...

THE DAY IN A FEW WORDS

DATE

WHAT DOES MY ...
NEED TODAY?

TODAY´S REASON FOR HAPPINESS

MIND

BODY

HEART

WHAT IS BOTHERING ME?

POSSIBLE
ACT OF SELF-LOVE

WHAT TO DO ABOUT IT TODAY?

I LIKE ABOUT MYSELF THAT ...

THE DAY IN A FEW WORDS

DATE

WHAT DOES MY ...
NEED TODAY?

TODAY'S REASON FOR HAPPINESS

MIND

BODY

HEART

WHAT IS BOTHERING ME?

POSSIBLE
ACT OF SELF-LOVE

WHAT TO DO ABOUT IT TODAY?

I LIKE ABOUT MYSELF THAT ...

THE DAY IN A FEW WORDS

DATE

WHAT DOES MY ...
NEED TODAY?

TODAY´S REASON FOR HAPPINESS

MIND

BODY

HEART

WHAT IS BOTHERING ME?

POSSIBLE
ACT OF SELF–LOVE

WHAT TO DO ABOUT IT TODAY?

I LIKE ABOUT MYSELF THAT ...

THE DAY IN A FEW WORDS

DATE

WHAT DOES MY ...
NEED TODAY?

TODAY'S REASON FOR HAPPINESS

MIND

BODY

HEART

WHAT IS BOTHERING ME?

POSSIBLE
ACT OF SELF-LOVE

WHAT TO DO ABOUT IT TODAY?

I LIKE ABOUT MYSELF THAT ...

THE DAY IN A FEW WORDS

DATE

WHAT DOES MY ...
NEED TODAY?

TODAY'S REASON FOR HAPPINESS

MIND

BODY

HEART

WHAT IS BOTHERING ME?

POSSIBLE
ACT OF SELF-LOVE

WHAT TO DO ABOUT IT TODAY?

I LIKE ABOUT MYSELF THAT ...

THE DAY IN A FEW WORDS

DATE

WHAT DOES MY ...
NEED TODAY?

TODAY'S REASON FOR HAPPINESS

MIND

BODY

HEART

WHAT IS BOTHERING ME?

POSSIBLE
ACT OF SELF-LOVE

WHAT TO DO ABOUT IT TODAY?

I LIKE ABOUT MYSELF THAT ...

THE DAY IN A FEW WORDS

SPACE FOR IDEAS